Alan Brownjohn was bor[n] primary and secondary sc[hool] 1953. At university he [ha]d be[en] generation of student poets [whi]ch included A. Alvarez, Anthony Thwaite, George MacBet[h], Geoffrey Hill, U. A. Fanthorpe, Adrian Mitchell, Jenny Joseph and Alistair Elliott. Since publishing his first full collection of poems, *The Railings* (1961), he has been an admired and influential presence in English poetry. Much anthologised, and at the same time difficult to fit into any one category or school, he has been characterised as belonging to a 'post-movement' tendency, as a poet who both learnt from and departed from the example of distinguished figures like Philip Larkin, Kingsley Amis and D. J. Enright, prominent in the famous 'Movement' of the 1950s. But his has always been an individual voice. There is a very particular sort of wit and precision, fantasy and sharp social awareness in all he writes.

As well as being a poet, Brownjohn has also been critic, teacher and promoter of poetry through organisations such as the Poetry Society, the Poetry Book Society and the Arvon Foundation, and in recent years has also produced classic drama translations (plays by Goethe and Corneille) and novels. His first novel, *The Way You Tell Them*, won the Authors' Club Award for the most promising first novel of its year (1990). That was followed by *The Long Shadows* (1997). The latest, his mordant comedy *A Funny Old Year* has just been published.

The Cat Without E-Mail, Brownjohn's tenth collection, once again displays every facet of his work – its humour, technical adeptness, and humanity. Alan Brownjohn divides his working time between London and Norfolk, and is a regular visitor to Romania, the setting for *The Long Shadows*.

ALAN BROWNJOHN

The Cat Without E-Mail

London
ENITHARMON PRESS
2001

First published in 2001
by the Enitharmon Press
36 St George's Avenue
London N7 0HD

Distributed by Littlehampton Book Services
through Signature Book Representation
2 Little Peter Street
Manchester M15 4PS

Distributed in the USA and Canada
by Dufour Editions Inc.
PO Box 7, Chester Springs
PA 19425, USA

ISBN 1 900564 57 2

Enitharmon Press gratefully acknowledges the
financial assistance of London Arts
and the Arts Council of England

British Library Cataloguing-in-Publication Data.
A catalogue record for this book is available
from the British Library.

Set in 10pt Plantin by Bryan Williamson, Frome,
and printed in Great Britain by
The Cromwell Press, Wiltshire

CONTENTS

S. L. B.
again

ACKNOWLEDGEMENTS

are due to the following, in which these poems or versions of them
originally appeared: *Acumen, Ambit, Around the Globe* (Journal of
the Shakespeare Globe Trust), British Council *New Writing*
anthologies, *Epoch* (USA), *Interchange, The Interpreter's House, Last
Words* (ed. Don Paterson and Jo Shapcott), *London Magazine,
London Review of Books, Orbis, Poetry London Newsletter, Poetry
Review, The Rialto, Spectator, Stand, Thumbscrew, Times Literary
Supplement, Turret Books*

THE CITIES

I was born in one of London's various cities,
And travelled through others that I never could
Explore except from an upper-deck front seat,
In the time I was a nineteen-thirties child.

Grown up from that, I learned to use the maps
Of more of them; but forgot to understand
What my own city told me, that outdated place
I thought I had left behind. When I go back now,

I can feel inside myself something waiting, hidden
By time and the Red Routes and the roundabouts,
By the deaths of faces I grew up among
And lost the strength to know.
                                        I like to think

– Or fear to think it – that one day my city will
Disclose itself, its faces reclaim their focus,
Its culverted rivers flood the hypermarkets,
The cinema organs rise through the motorways.

POEM ABOUT MEN

Thing about girls was, they were everywhere!
They lived above furniture shops, alighted on
Your field of vision in recreation grounds,
And licked ice-creams by corner-shop entrances,
And sat in groups in the very same seats each day
Of the first bus home the moment school came out.
They could be the daughters of plumbers, or officers
In local government, or sit two rows in front
In the Regal, and you'd never seen *them* before.
There could be girl cousins with them, or friends who'd come
From a distant town, and you thought, *Please don't go back!*

Women are different, though, living with local
Government officers, married to plumbers, leaving
Cars on rainy superstore parking places,
With hardened furrows set in their twenty
-Nine year old faces; complicit in mortgages,
With futures on too-fragile salary scales.
I believe that women have never been girls at all,
Just women from the start, kept somewhere else
When the streets were full of girls from everywhere
– And finally released to do away
With girls for their lack of brutal obviousness,
Girls for their courage in being unusual,
Girls for their cheek in being their younger selves.

THREE 'O' POEMS

1. A Defence of Reading

O in the spring the legs were out,
  And they were smooth and trim,
And every eye that saw them felt
  They must be out for him.

O in the spring the legs were out,
  And they were cold and pure,
And chastised the ambitions of
  The eyes that felt so sure

– But they declined to play the game
  The proud legs had begun,
And they could stare down anything
  Faster than legs could run.

Therefore the summer saw the legs
  Give up their cold disguise,
And sun themselves to frazzles for
  The catching of the eyes;

And thus it was the bolder eyes
  Could stare down easily
The flimsy ramparts of the legs,
  And have their victory,

Have it, have it and tire of it
  Much sooner than they thought,
And spend the autumn brooding on
  The truth the legs had taught:

That love is not as hard-won or
  As worthwhile as it looks,
And those that tell you differently
  Have only stared at books.

11

2. *Ars Poetica*

O here we go a-gathering
    The samphire from the crannies,
Inside the little baskets woven
    For us by our grannies.

Two hundred feet below, the rocks,
    And up above, the spaces,
And here the wind that thumps us while
    The rain runs down our faces.

Yet still we edge down clutching
    Special clippers to collect it,
Hoping to find it hanging out
    Where no one would expect it,

Looking to catch it unawares,
    All richly green, and blooming
Within our fingers' nimble grasp,
    Before it sees us coming.

If gathering rosebuds should be quite
    A profitable doddle,
And nuts in May might sell O.K.,
    Our samphire brings in sod-all;

But following daily such a dread-
    ful trade to earn a living,
With every second on that cliff
    So cruel and unforgiving,

Is fine – as long as no one comes
    And asks us what we do there . . .
We'd have to say, Without our toil,
    Just who would know it grew there?

3. *Against Mathematics*

O Sod sits up there on his bench,
    And when things are just awful,
Throws down some extra lumps of mud
    Pretending that it's lawful.

But though Sod's Law is petty, and
    Productive of frustrations,
In its odd way it does permit
    Of kindly deviations:

Where mathematics says *Man dies*
    Like all the other fauna,
Sod's quirky Law says *Live some more,*
    There's trouble round the corner.

Old Sod is sly but jocular
    – Plain fact and not a rumour –
But Maths by definition works
    Without a sense of humour;

And whereas Sod chucks mud with no
    Fixed rules for hour or season,
Maths functions logically by
    The ruthless clock of reason.

There is no mercy ever for
    The ones who starve in attics,
Victims of the inexorable
    Laws of mathematics,

But Sod at least has idle days
    When he provides some quarter
– And makes a happier study for
    Your able son; or daughter.

O superfluous sprays of light on an esplanade!
The winter urn is cooling, the girl is closing:
I'm sorry, she says, *We are closing now.*

– But the customer asks about tea with such hope-less charm
That the girl is not resentful she cannot
Go home quite yet; perhaps go home any more.

This one can charm the birds down from the trees
So they thud to the ground in dozens, and the girl
Is second by second feeling wingless

– And she drops down behind the counter, behind
The fridge of coloured ices, small plastic skips
Full of scraped-at choices of lime, or tangerine,

Or rum-and-raisin. It drones while he drums his fingers
(Little finger up to thumb) and smiles and smiles.
The girl lies there and thinks, *Do I have a choice?*

With my head against the cartons of UHT?
With my eyes trapped by shelves lined by newspapers
Full of photographs of terrors I hadn't really

Ever noticed 'til this moment, one leg straight out,
One leg bent under, one thin arm free to move?
Could I lie here and hope he leaves, and closes

The door? she wonders. *I shall know if he's gone*
When the bell rings. Or should I push
The panic button, fast, for living help?

Or should I serve him? Over the sea, the sun
Goes through the bottom-line horizon, far away,
Below three colour-choices of January cloud.

A WITNESS

Did something drop down and move out over the shore,
Just now? In front of, then lost to sight in, the mist?
The colours in the perspective tell me nothing.
Did something occur that the light would not yield up?

– That was the final question of the day,
The seascape as usual resigned to dull entropy,
No spaced-out clouds forming up into glowing processions,
No cinematic gloriousness and hope.

– It might for a moment have been something falling there.
The day had begun, and was ending, blank. But at four-
Fifteen was there an unobserved low-tide success?
An Icarus landing on sand, getting up and running?

THROWBACK

Ridiculous no one told them they could stop:
At the extreme end of a corridor
Was the ballroom of what was a Grand Hotel,
Sold and left to the weather to shut it down.
I could curiously hear as we walked along it
(I and somebody else who might have been
Any one, I suppose, of a number of friends)
Certain amplified sounds. more amplified by echoes.
Turning out to be music. Surely it couldn't be
An orchestra still at it? It could be the wind?

But there, when we walked in over the fallen door
And across the plaster fallen from the ceiling
(As on one night of my early adolescence,
When I followed, at her suggestion, Dolores O'Leary,
Her real name, on VE-night, in Sportsbank Hall
As a flying bomb had left it) were a bride and a groom
Still dancing, still dressed in their wedding stuff.
To see them now, circling round, looking over
Each other's shoulders, didn't seem quite right.
Nor did their calling to me by *my* real name.

MOSQUITO

Fancy this in October, the last
Mosquito of summer left buzzing alone,
Its last fling in my room on the sixth floor
Of a tower block hotel; marooned like one
In his seventh decade with only the past
To look forward to, as the one sure

Topic he can buzz round with some old chum.
'I had a good bloody summer,' it seems to say,
'With waiter and bellman, and that prim peach
Who keeps the consultant's books across the way.'
And for one last sally it swoops and bites my thumb.
So I bite mine back at it, and reach

For a folded newspaper; all the same aware
How much I resemble it, my own small spites
And hopeless needs reduced to the last fling
Of one who doles out charm in sexless bites
To check-out girls and bank clerks as if to swear,
'Oh man, I buzz and suck like anything!'

SUMMER TIME ENDS

How nice looking up, some cloudy afternoon,
To see that what has fallen suddenly
Is twilight, and an earlier chance to draw
The curtains while you have the energy.

Now everything falls, go down with it and give
Yourself to the gravity, putting up a show
Of warming wistfulness with the last leaves.
Fall hard, and stay there, waiting for the snow.

The nights are drawing in, nothing wrong with that.
The poet says: *Darkness cures what day inflicts.*
It is as normal to welcome winter back
As to loathe the spring. Popular interdicts

May forbid that preference, but snow walks are like
Illicit love with no one else betrayed;
Are like the joy, as you step out through the white,
Of the first alligator in the first everglade.

Harden your skin, then, for the rigorous spell
Between October and the April days
When the clocks go wrong again. Live for the thought
Of the bracing dark and the heavenly displays,

On frosty nights, of dotty groups of stars
You may sit and try to specify all night
– As if there were no tomorrow to dissolve
Their shining in dull anywheres of light.

SEVENS FOR GAVIN EWART

(1916–1995)

Something Audenesque for a conclusion?
  In dignified, indented, limestone lines?
But in Wystan's geology hills were permanent,
  Whereas human geography constantly changes,
That being its only constancy. We reach plateaux in life
  When friends seem likely always to be there,
Changeless features in the landscape. And then –

  There are places in poetry where nothing seems
Appropriate to write after the sudden dash
  Suggesting an interruption, or a shock:
The words halt dumbstruck in the mind, in blankness
  Of a sort you never showed. You had six days left.
Sat upright in a chair in the too-warm ward,
  You were checking proofs: 'I'm not on my last legs –

'I've work to do,' you affirmed, with the stern expression
  Reserved for the moments when you took exception
To some shabby behaviour or rotten rhyming.
  That look could be unexpected, the touchstone suddenly
Revealed that made you mentor as well as friend,
  Our example of someone never speechless in verse,
Never letting words fail you, or work remain unfinished –

  Like your final quatrain, done on a day when 'not much
Poetry was coming', and putting the old and their carers
  Firmly in their place with rueful sentiments
Adapting Lewis Carroll. Seventy-nine
  Is 21 years longer than the average
Male could expect to live when I was 11
  (The NHS, we believed). Poets don't, these days –

Another wise thought of yours – need to push their careers
  By dying young. But cell and virus and blood-clot
Might have waited in some cases until four score
  (You had six years of the Second War, and then
Two decades of silence). And surely given us,
  For a little longer, your memory: of the famous
Far younger than we saw them, and of course –

  The legendary dead. E.g., Mr Yeats arriving
Late for *Sweeney Agonistes* in an attic theatre,
  Treading fatefully up the stairs to stand in the doorway
In cloak and hat as if he was some part
  Of the performance. Our memories, Gavin,
Will retain your own appearances at parties,
  Standing, as you preferred, in some quieter corner –

Forever Ewart's! The last time we talked at one,
  It was prosody, *New Verse*, and the Café Royal
We discussed, not conglomerate managers twitching
  The strings on which their puppets dance for cake . . .
With disgraceful energy you assured me this calling
  Was still the best; all your faith was firm in it.
– We'll try to keep that as we grieve and smile.

TEMPER, TEMPER

I chase a bug around a tree,
I'll have his blood, he knows I will!
– And yet the tree forestalls me with
The thought of all the chlorophyll

Flowing into those gentle leaves
That spread themselves above my head;
And so I cease to chase the bug,
And rest my aches and pains instead

Beneath its shade; and pass an hour
Where I can find tranquillity
With ample space for man and beast
– Comprising both the bug and me.

Of course I know that this bug took,
For sustenance, or on a whim,
Some blood from me, five minutes past,
But *need* I take some back from him?

In any case it might be mine,
And I shan't need it anyway:
It's hardly worth expense of spite
On such a genial summer's day.

Instead I'll pluck a shiny leaf,
Which, if he likes, the bug may take,
And thank me, as the equal of
The Buddha, or of William Blake.

WRONG DAY

So now: lifted smoothly and quietly upwards alone
In the cubic warmth to an unalterable
Arrival at the penthouse floor; for company,
My hair to comb fast in the mirror behind me;
My shoulders to stiffen, but then to relax;
My mouth muscles rehearsing a good smile.
And who isn't honoured by chunky doors opening
On such a carpeted perspective stretching out –

Each step on its fitted verdure reassuring,
Each name and number clear on the passing doors?
Until at the last door Mr Macpherson – having
Measured the time I would need from Reception to here –
Has opened it wide, five paces before I arrive.
He insists I step inside in front of him,
And that I sit in his chair at his cleared desk
While he stands; and nods he is ready for my decisions.

THE RASSENDYLL SERVICE

No longer in the schedules. But you still see it
Through the proper binoculars at the right moment,
Laying down cylinders of steam for the off-sea winds
To disperse when it has passed; lighting tonight
The necklines of bays facing east before it veers
Inland across plains to where cities of porn shops, cathedrals,
Statues and archives solidify others' dreams.
Its passengers are always mysteries (the past
Will have seen to that) with an aura of being claimants
To whatever is impossible elsewhere.

At none of the junctions it stops at does anyone
Leave or join it, it stays proudly self-contained
And amazing to the gaze of excluded travellers
In small-hours stations. At dawn, a railwaywoman
On a country platform whirls on the end of a chain
An irrelevant key, while a young guard makes to wipe
A crumb from her lapel; and see, she smiles
A permissory smile you take in from your corner seat:
A cameo of unrehearsed perfection.
But they do not halt this train, and it moves onwards

Past even smaller halts where they reassure you,
With crimson sleeves horizontal in salute,
That everything in the kingdom is in order.
Then comes the last slowing-up, to the terminus
In the heart of your fantasy: a marvellous mayor,
As archetypal as the bishop with him
– Each renewed in his office for just this occasion –
Is welcoming you on the concourse, to drive you up
To the Metacontinental Hotel on Citadel Hill.
You sign the book with a gold pen you may keep.

At the threshold of the lift you feel the pressure
Of his hand of power on the shoulders of your suit.
He himself now closes the pantographic doors
And smiles you away and up, all gracious
Knowingness . . .
                        Then you're raising your head from where
You lay face downwards with someone on *such* pillows,
And recall that all the foregoing was how you got here,
That cryptic dangers wait outside the door,
That you haven't remembered the code word for going back
– Though meanwhile you look up, and above the bed-board

Is a picture of a great old train coming out of a tunnel.

THREE WAYS WITH KITES

Close-up: the handling of, the words about
How kites can be handled, practical talk
On when to tug less, or more, the stuff of string
And hooks; also how you need to walk
With good judgement of the breeze, when you turn to bring
A different angle to their flight without
Causing them to swoop down and slap the turf.

With fine eye-glasses you can stand farther off,
Subsume the exercise of skills, and wait
For the chance of any beauty you could remark
In one particular kite: look how it soars
With that red tail rippling figures of eight
To paint the clouds that watch the public park.

Back home, use kites when you want metaphors.

SHE

The latest conclusion: *Drink* is rapidly
Acquiring a me problem. The girl I presume
Most of any day to follow, but don't meet at all
– Last thing at night she is actually in the room
As the large hours shift into the small,
Sitting over there and (*Sex* is obsessed with me)
Watching these lines take their particular
Shape as my latest tentative report
On all that she means; laughing too readily
While the halo of my table lamp stops short
Of her hair, which would indisputably
Shine with it, if it could ever reach that far.

WHAT SHE REQUIRED

No use imagining better things to do,
The chance of finding those will have gone already.
    Is a gale blowing up? It certainly is.
It lifts the tiles off the roofs and breaks
    The casements open. Were they so unsteady,
The walls of this romantic pledge you knew
    Might never be fulfilled? Something that always takes
Huge luck and costs you tiresome agonies

    Over all the trivia which might be turned
Into golden keys . . . ?
                        No, look! Today
    Is the day you waited for. Though in fifty years
The wind has howled each sheltering grown-up tree
    Into contortions, you at least can say
There are leaves growing on them, and the grass has earned
    Those deer now chewing it contentedly.
It is a summer when she reappears,

    And you, waiting statue, see her move back again
Into your field of vision, walk towards this place
    From a direction only you were free
To imagine, on a path only you two share,
    Her dress and purpose your own choice, her face
Whatever shape you hoped it might retain
    – Yet entering not by a ceremonial stair,
But by a side-door and quite silently.

OVERVIEW FROM AN EMBANKMENT

Two fifty-year olds, on their own – and a goal each?
I watch them from the stopped train . . . Must be some duel
They are acting out: the big thin bloke, out of reach,
Running hard, and the other chasing; who then, with a cruel
Tackle takes the ball, dribbles fast to the far far end,
All the time pursued by his slow loping scarecrow friend

Who is there first, naturally. His arms, long sticks,
Wave wildly in the goal to reduce its space
As he challenges this side and that; so his partner kicks
Too timidly, and this keeper falls with his face
Pressed hard on the ball, he loves it, he hoists it hard past
The other and gallops to follow it fast

– And so it goes on, and on, in that dusk of the day
Between six thirty-nine and about six fifty-eight,
When you can't really tell if people you're seeing may
Have had their tea, or haven't; and the light
Shining down on this pitch is like their faded
Back kitchen light when only a jaded

Glow stays on, over mangle and draining-board
Where the last groove wet from the stacked-up dinner plates
Has dried, and the air secretes a not-to-be-ignored
Pale radiance, like this courage of two old mates
Regarding life at fifty as much the same
Set of futile chances as their boyhood game.

SONNET AT SIXTY-FOUR

You think of the various things you've never done,
Like going to Greenland, or riding a horse
– Which is unlikely now, though you confess
That if well paid to play Kutuzov . . . And wasn't there one
Great idea you used to have, now of course
Too late to try for: a dignified progress,
Serving an honourable government,
To the House of Lords, relaunched with a different name?

Only yesterday I thought, Come to that, you've never spent
A few measly quid to have an epigram
Or a picture done in the form of a tattoo
On . . . some suitable organ. So I stopped on a yellow line
And scanned the small shop-window. And read this sign
– At last, the AIDS-free needle – here – for *you!*

THE BARON'S HORSE

So there was I, woken up on the airy height
Of an eighty-foot steeple by my master – the story goes –
Shouting up at me from below, *We must move on!*
It's eight o'clock, and we must be moving on,
And you're stuck up there tied to a past when the snows
Of faith were at the full – ten o'clock last night!

'But I'm happier here,' I neighed back, as my hoofs
Slid, and grappled at the slates, 'I've known far worse
Dilemmas and qualms than this, this feels like comfort
To a horse who has seen and suffered, it's more like
        comfort –'
I have the ultimate shit-scared, fundamental horse,
It seems! he thundered. Drips dropped from all the roofs

As he ranted with no regard for *my* situation,
Some eighty comforting feet above the town,
Still slithering after the thought of the one God,
Or any available prophet of the one God
– Until, with a shot, my master brought me down
To his earth again; and to pure imagination.

DOGS

She was only a postman's daughter, but . . .
She was only a publican's daughter, but . . .
She was only a tobacconist's daughter, but . . .

She was only a lighthousekeeper's daughter . . .
– They had what it takes, and it seems the world allowed
Them to use it. Were their humble fathers proud?

Did their daughters learn it from them, take after them?
Or were their girls defying them, getting blamed
For leaving those old men bitter and ashamed?

What of their mothers? We are never told
Which way, if any, they wanted their girls to go.
What part *they* played we never get to know.

Their mothers were like dogs that never barked
When footfalls fell during nights as black as ink.
What kept them quiet? Whose daughters were they, do you think?

ELEGIACS ON A PIER

Only thin planks over the frayed processional
Of white-green waves; and walking, it's possible to prop
One's body up with the wind swaying out-of-season rows
Of unlit, coloured bulbs as if they were skipping ropes,
But made of electric wires.
                              From the vantage-point of the pier,
The town takes up its old Edwardian stand on the cliffs,
Insisting that pleasure and health can still combine here as when,
Before Shangri-La and Atlantis were sold in packages, chartered,
Gentility arrived in the high horseless carriages
They mounted mudguards into, as they had into those pulled by
    horses.
The sea is just as bracing, and even some views of the town
Are what one's grandfather saw . . .
                              But matters like music and crime
Are updated now. The radio, stood on the café shelf
Beyond the 'Home Made Pastries' displayed in plastic foil,
Thunders a cruder love song, then announces that *a man
Has been found guilty of selling drugs to schoolgirls at a school gate,
And will be sentenced tomorrow.*
                              A red-bloused manageress
With shiny stockings walks by, and receives some feedback from
The young boy serving coffee in mugs from a screaming urn,
While the wind that controls our lives clears everything away,
The spume on the beach, the litter, a pedestrian's antique hat
– All of this seen through the swing-door when it opens onto the
    blast
And the vertical lines of the planks all hurl themselves towards
The slopes of the town where the church, with its restored red
    brick
Crowns the huddle of red bed-and-breakfasts that live on around
    its spire.
Those all match her scarlet blouse as she answers the boy, 'Oh
    ri-i-ght!'
And her walk across the floor is dignified and correct,
While the sea below goes on presenting propositions

32

Which the beach accepts with patience.

                          All of this, she and I, and the boy,
And a no-doubt familiar man who comes striding into the place
To order 'A flapjack and tea' in a wild falsetto voice,
A daily habit – we are all sentenced, whatever our plans,
Like the criminal peddling drugs to the chattering girls at the gate;
Though the manageress later on, in quite another role,
As lover not manageress, may say, 'You may stroke my thigh
If you promise not to stop there.'

                     The cliffs running out to the west
Dwindle down along the shore, perspective works like that,
Yet increase on the horizon, quite logically because
They are much higher one mile away than they are in front of the
     pier
– And it's this perpetual trick that phenomena seem to achieve
Of being unexpected that makes it hard to bear
The sentence we are under.

                 Because, if everything
Were regular and the same, if routines never changed,
We might bow our heads and say when the time arrived, 'It's
     enough,
I'll go quietly.' But this is a world that constantly alters and shifts,
The sea casting up other gravel, the mad falsetto man
Going absent for a day, then turning up to demand
'Coffee and baked beans on toast' on Thursday that makes you
     resent
The fact that it has to go, that the end-of-September blinds
Must finally clatter down and darken the sea's great stage
– And worse, exclude you from it.

                    Yes, deny you your corner seat
On which, a week or so later, the sun could be shining so hard
That your coffee might heat up again, the page after page that you
     write
Make luminous sense after all, and the red-bloused manageress
Stroll across with a different idea, mere stranger though you may
     be,
Like a cliff increasing again. And not in the distance now.

STREAM

In the key-cutting shop I thought of the following:
The scream of a key being cut as representing

The pain of opening dangerous doors onto . . . Where?
Then the thought of someone beyond one door, sat there

Expecting my intrusion, it being no shock
As my sudden arrival via a changed lock

Had been anticipated for several years . . .
Next there comes on stream an image of what appears

To be a hand I raise to my lips to kiss,
On the other side of the coffee line; and in this,

As I release the hand, and it falls back
Not-so-slowly to her side, I can see the slack

Downward tilt of the Second World towards
The Third, something surely that accords

With the maxims of Harvard. Thus, obviously,
The ambivalent smiling face the key had brought me

Was proposing a joint venture I should decline,
And the tannoy sound of a conscience I knew was mine

Said: Take the key from the machine, leave it uncut
Leave the door, wherever it might be, silent, shut,

And imagine the ethnic proverb might speak true:
Before bash down brickwork think of polluted view.

SEVEN SHERLOCKS

The man on the bus to the beach was Chinese.
He was certainly not. He was disguised
As a Chinese. Did you not see how he read
His little Li-Po edition from front to back?

But the only prints on the sand were those
Of a horse. – Or those left by a tall man
Taking careful strides with horseshoes attached
To the soles of cheap wellington boots.

So the third man in the saltmarsh was never
– *There at all?* Quite. Was never there at all.
Because he did not relax his guard and walk
Away. He stood still. He was a scarecrow.

And there was nothing wrong with the old red kiosk
Outside the village store. *But I think there was!*
No! Briggs was standing in it using
His mobile phone to *persuade* us that there was.

All that nodding and shaking of his bald head
At what Carstairs was saying . . . – Yes, messages
To his accomplice on the distant dunes.
He could do nothing when the sun went in.

And the vital missing *element, just*
As important as the rest? – The absence
Of a haystack near the gate. Had one been there,
He would have shoved our needle into it.

Then, you see, those clouds . . . They were *painted* on the sky
In the manner of the artist Magritte.
– *But how could you tell?* – On longer inspection,
I found crucial errors in the forgery.

A SONG OF SURROGATE STREET

It was a downtown restaurant, certainly,
But not so grand; where one night I sat drinking
– Myself and a shabby figure at Number Six –
When I sensed, in the semi-gloom, a waitress thinking,
About that character, she and I could see
Him staring at her, 'Don't like his little tricks,

'He thinks he can get away with them in the mirror,
But I make sure he knows I can see him there
When I glance at him myself, and over his book
He's giving me that nasty smiling stare
Which he hopes I might respond to; an error
Of judgement, if you ask me . . . Oh, men can look

'If they want to, I'm not one to create a fuss,
But I prefer to choose myself who's to have
The right to, and who's not.' – Then I thought I heard
The man silently responding: 'I do believe
That if I keep my head down and quietly use
The corner of my eye while I sit and read,

'I shall catch her staring absently this way,
Or pretending it's absently, as she turns and brings
My omelette from the hatch, my mineral,
My roll with no butter, and other harmless things.'
– And this goes on at seven fifteen every day,
The man sat at Number Six so as to fall

Under the cold attentions of the girl;
And the girl who consents to be lonely in the end,
And because she is lonely one day starts staring too,
Thinking his stare might be her only friend,
Also the stares will seem comfortingly less real
For being in a mirror. They will meet through

Their images only, in a silent act
Of recognition agreed out of a distress
Neither admits to, face to silvered face
Communing in a proxy happiness . . .
And for some weeks will maintain their secret pact,
Though the other mirrors repeat it all round the place.

THE INVITATION

I used to prefer, when walking, measuring a distance
And then turning back, not taking a wide circle.

But today I did the circle instead, and returned
To the clouded-over start from another direction

– And there was my path striking off across rainy fields
Without the resigned look of somewhere I had covered

Two times over. I recognised its attractions,
I had proved them already. I could almost hear it say,

You can see I am clean of your original footprints
Which I closed over like water as you walked on.

The relevant circumstances have been rethought.
The hidden sun is higher now, two hours later.

I have changed in that time. So might you. Start over again?

RISK-TAKERS

Bad day, forecast *Sultry*, the flag
On the pole above the Russian
Roulette Club in the High Street limp,
Their bar shut, its blinds drawn, too few
Proven fatalities lately
To attract new members.
                              Try *Life*
Instead? With some rival outfit
Like *Aerobic Death Restriction*?
Well, you could all the same end up
With a craving for risk – years lost
You could have glutted on it.
                              No,
Cross the High Street, and take a look.
On the door of that place it says
Pleasant club requires risk-takers
Less gone on money than seeking
The hazards of high art.
                              The gun,
Primed by Amanda, Natalie,
Cindy (whoever's on duty
On the fateful week-end) has *pen*,
Or *stave*, *brush* or *chisel* sprayed in
Blood, sperm or tears on its barrel.
On the wall in the corner of
The agonized back saloon where
The baize table stands, among pinned
Banknotes with the price on each face,
You might find Benjamin Franklin
Looking jealous on his greenback:
The frown of power, yes; but scared white.

FACIAL

Inaccurate foray, in front of the bathroom mirror,
With blunt scissors angled too awkwardly near the eyes,
That see an infinite snow of hairs spread across
The sheet of white cardboard held widely under my chin . . .

I tap the edge of the card with the closed blades,
And all the hairs shift together like filings pulled
Into sentient activity by a magnet.
Dropped into the bathroom basin they cluster and clog

The outlet like a dampened pubic bush,
A mesh that looks wiry enough to scour the bowl with.
I pick up this excrement, a grey-brown ball
To flush, or dump in a bin, when I have finished;

But I can't say how long that will take, say how much longer
I should spare to go on attempting to reach a state
When I look just trim and suitable; not, as now,
More exposed and less composed than when I started.

SONNET IN SLOPPY JOE'S

A red-bead message runs all along the wall:
For the Best American Breakfast the Flame
-Grilled Burger, This is the PLACE. Lids of some tall
Coffee-pots with chrome knobs on look much the same
As Kaiser Wilhelm helmets; they don't make sense,
But they've used them by filling them up half-way
With clusters of coffee-bags, like a pretence
Of fungi on trees.   And soon that girl will say,
'Mum, did you see that Tammy Wynette had died?
What will Grandma think?' – 'Oh, she knows already,
She heard it on the 6 a.m. news. She cried,
And said, "I think I'll have a glass of sherry."
But six is much too early for sherry, Mum.
"Not for me", she said. "Not for me." And she *had* some.'

BURIAL OF 5-7-5

He had often said about secrets, 'When you dare
To give one away, the hearer's never grateful, you yourself
Are condemned in the information you devalue.'

But today is the opened umbrella,
Black and dry in the bath above downstairs talk, low-toned,
Concerning a safe route afterwards to lunch.

In both the wing-mirrors in the middle lane
All the cars we see are the same, or compatible, colours; through
The windscreen we only catch the hearse.

At the perilous gates, in the chapel, no one
Admits a personal link with these transactions, we are there
To dissociate ourselves, and respond to music.

We stare out the cemetery wind. Some stumble
Around the wound in the earth, but reach hands to the shoulders
Of others stumbling with mud on their hands.

On the road again: 'Did you pick up a pamphlet?
"Society for the Unexpected Enhancement of Flowers?" Or this:
"Sex Now, or in the Hereafter? A Debate"?'

In the restaurant, pegs for balaclavas, and the lovely
Virgin he discovered on that last night (with her death's-head
earrings)
Recurring with an Air Vice-Marshal not her father.

Then the bill, put down in a leather-cased
Limited edition of the manager's elegies . . . And the waiter's silver
Bangle sliding down to his knuckle bones.

ONE YEAR TODAY

Those days in summer when we condescended
To stay at the Summer Palace . . . They didn't turn out
As we assumed they might from the name it had.
Sunshine was rare. We shivered. And there's no doubt

That the days in winter when we reportedly
Enjoyed the Winter Palace, frankly those
Were scarcely frozen enough for the name to apply.
We perspired in humid mists. There were no snows.

As for spring and autumn, they did not require
Their own palaces. They were more ambivalent
Than even the other two seasons. So we swanned through power
With pretend-demarcations. Government

Was in the minds of the governed, made-over faces
And resolute postures suggesting a firm, a nice,
Distinction between right and wrong.
                                      And tell me, who raises
Banners when imprecision looks so precise?

EU

In my dream, a new dream, I still have some,
I was in the Apennines – where I haven't been;
I'd in fact been to the cinema and home to sleep
In the Carpathians – in this dream I'd come,
After slogging up some foothills admiring the scene,
To a small mountain hut, no more than a heap
Of stones flung together to keep the winter out . . .
I stood there, and gave a loud unanswered shout.
Inside not, as in the film I'd seen, a wall
With a shepherd's family photograph; instead
A new London tube map pinned up, with a small
Arrow aimed at 'Bank'; and above, in day-glo red,
The words of a less-than-cryptic message: 'All
Your life, wherever you are, YOU WILL BE HERE', it said.

ON MY 66TH BIRTHDAY

The speeding of footsteps, and the shouting
Up an outside stair: the siren race begun
To break down a fire-door and enter. Someone
Locked in to be rescued? Some thing
Occurred there too late to forestall it?
The rumours breed in our block, opposite,
As duty hurries to the place, its hard
Boots and fire-axes and counsellors
Always ready to act on these sudden clamours

. . . One day it will be there *before* the word
Has formed in the head, and long before the key
Has been clicked in the lock. The emergency
Call will have been, yes, spotted in advance
Pulsating on the screen of the Guaranteed
Death Prevention Unit: *You have all you need*
With your sheet of peel-off stickers. Take no chance,
There are plenty for whenever you want them, to keep
In your wallet, desk diary, car. Awake. Asleep.

AVALANCHE DOGS

At a whistling instruction from its trainer,
The little dog leapt at the large bank of snow,
Sniffed and barked and scratched, and its trainer helped it,
And through a hole they made the crowd could see
A face, that soon turned out to be Mrs Sundquist's.

My cat, and all my previous cats, have warned me
Against giving undue respect to any dog
Or credence to its talents. Did I listen too much?
This dog was thrown things for showing off its flair,
Though not many people seemed to value the sacrifice

Donated by Mrs Sundquist, who was covered
With snow again for a second dog to find her
– All this being done to show the ability
Of avalanche dogs to get Mrs Sundquist,
Or you or me perhaps, out of mountain snows,

In this case in the Lappland Arctic region,
Where every husky in the dog-sled teams
Knows left from right . . . And a third dog, and a fourth,
Mrs Sundquist being buried and reburied
Time and time again in the square outside People's House,

And people applauding the dogs, yet not Mrs Sundquist
When she finally came out from her hour-long incarceration
In the twilight drift.
          I clapped my own soft gloves,
And one or two others took up the applause
– But which of us had brought anything to throw

To Mrs Anna Sundquist, dog's best friend?

DUTY POEM

Avoiding the cluttered table, I pause awkwardly.
It isn't the gift of the image of August snow
Threading through the foreground steam that rises now
From the drink held to my lips. And it's not,
This time, from just a pleasure in pausing. But
Because I have seen one truth concerning Duty

– It need not be an escarpment one has decided
To draw deliberate breaths for, about to see
If muscles and sinews have the energy.
And it isn't so much the case of having to set
Aside some advantage one plotted for months to get.
It's the tiny inertias that ought to be roused and tidied

– And when that's done – Mankind! Such a flat
Smooth, emptied table-top is within one's range . . .
Was ever anything so clean, clear, strange
-ly resolute? Stretching for miles in front of the eyes
Without reproach, or guilt, or compromise?
. . . And you wish, you wish, you wish it would stay like that.

TREES NEAR PODORAS

Not the same week every autumn, but the same
Place and surprise: clouds and clouds all day,
At six made over to encroaching dark
– And then this avenue which, for a spell,
We have driven along (planted by Communists
With the decent motive, that time, of providing
A windbreak on a windy plain) suddenly
Lights up our way through the dying afternoon,
As the breeze blows, turns, and flattens the leaves
On their yellow sides, so they provide a wide
Gold illumination, a rush of light.
                                        It gives
A ceremonial radiance to a road
Which once more looks as if it still might offer
A future with possibilities. So does
The instinctive raised thumb of liberal well-wishing
From the shepherd, returning our wave of thanks
When he barred his bleating gang for our car to pass,
Folding down at the end into a fist of hope.

GRAIN

Today sun, frost – and restlessness.
                    Room to room
I walked with my friend and our clinging shadows reached
Right out to the walls. But in the cellar's gloom
They couldn't find us, so we went untouched
Down the steps to look in a sheen of water,
Seeped in from the lake. At its edge – unsteady –
Shivering – I stopped. I sensed that ice might cover
Even these reflections soon, as the day turned cloudy,
And – *December*, I reflected, *month of my first*
Clear memory of winter . . .
                   Back then, as well,
Shadows clung to us, boy and friend, dispersed
As we slipped them in the cellar. Skies were set to fall,
Exactly as today. Now too, I'll go
Back up alone to walk the road outside,
Take the touches of the dizzying dots of snow
On my held-out hand, think of loves and dreads and angers
As I did at seven.
                Frost and snow, unchanged, abide.
All that alters is the grain of my outstretched fingers.

1999, 1939

ON HUNGERFORD BRIDGE

'I am sorry, but just now Mr Macpherson is
[Where you are shut out like a draught from the world,

At the polished prairie of a tabletop
Where no call from outside is ever taken,

And savouring a conclave you cannot join,
Moving other people's goalposts] in a meeting.'

What the caller has down there on the raining bridge
Is the undeniable right to shift a carrier

From one cut hand to the other and scrawl
Illegally in felt tip in the dusk

An addendum to the graffito on the advert
The world is in a [FUCK YOU] meeting. 'I shan't

'Call back,' he says. He has no goalpost,
Only the knowledge of air on a living face.

THE NOSTALGIA EXPERIENCE

What a great idea!
          – Yes, an entire block, shelf on shelf
Of rentable double rooms. And here, the one your
Own card was swiped for, a payment which guarantees
Your admission as a *bona fide* user
Of the past. In those squares you inked in were
Print-outable names and authentic memories
Which someone else would complement on their own sheet
– And already tonight, in Room No. 444,
Is a distant name who filled in for you, *yourself!*

Old newspapers line the drawers, the same harmonics
Of empty hangers are sounding tremblingly,
In tune with the underground trains. All that it needs
Is this feel of candlewick, the nylon pillow,
And one further thing, that lamp outside the window
No curtains ever shut out . . .
                    As each hour leads
Slowly back into the next, there's *your* chance to meet
In a virtual past; and touch where there used to be
Erogenous zones . . . Infallible mnemonics.

LIFE FORCE

She'll be coming round the mountain when she comes
– But will she? If you think about it, she'd
Be perfectly entitled to opt for some brand new
Route we'd never dreamt of. So, let's proceed
To other unasked questions: Why should her coming
Deserve to be sung? And who is she anyway?
                                        Just humming
The tune at home, and trying to think it through,
One sees there is more to ponder than one assumes
When bawling it lost in the fens, or at the station
While striving to keep warm and show a brave face
In the hope of a last train, and its affirmation
'That life goes on, with all its small certainties,
Its fixed feasts and timetables still in place . . .
But whatever else divides it, the world agrees
That 'she' must be coming. And of course her style
Of clothing, that's crucial, it's shamefully worse
Wearing jeans than pink pyjamas; and her route
Must lie in this direction, and there's no doubt
That she is coming soon.
                        But we'll have her drive one horse
(Not six of them), up a valley from the south;
(Not 'round the mountain') on a road that lets you see
Her approaching faster, faster on the last mile
In a maddened gallop. And finally she'll get down
And crash through the swing doors to greet us hated youth
In our favourite bar – a life force. Dick the Clown,
Bill the Mogg, Shining Tony, Sturdy John
Up there at their high-level tables, and hardly one
Among that crowd as clever as he thought
– To whom she will declare, 'Choose death – or *me*!
Look, boys – the ball is bouncing in *your* court.'

DRESSING

The first pit of the day. A moment
When the hole in a much-worn life is like
A hole in the pocket of what I'd intended to wear
To leap over that, a gap down which
Certain things had dropped which I'd stored not
Remembering – pens, peppermints, paper-clips
– Three aspirins put down as deposits on
Anxiety-free hours – my Membership Card –
And look, 50p! With all of these in my hand,
I reviewed the stretch ahead: unpromising,
But coloured with small surprises now, didn't
They shine, too. Were there hopes in the margins
I suddenly could see my existence was framed in?
It would need to be tested.
                              I set them out,
These reserves, on the table before I open the curtains:
A scarecrow army sentried against daylight.

ANTONIO: AN EPILOGUE

The company, I am very pleased to say,
Has survived a troubled year in excellent shape
To face the challenge of the global market.
The rebrand and relaunch under the name
'Sea Pageants plc', with the support
Of capital accruing from court proceedings
(More of which in a moment) has been successful.

Safety checks on all vessels have revealed
No fault in any, though I would accept
That communications technology needs improvement.
(The captain of one ship, the *Enterprise*,
Remains suspended on full pay, pending
The apprehension of the two Moorish sailors
Responsible for its loss on the Goodwin Sands.)

The most serious threat to us during the year
Was, of course, the attempt at a corporate raid
By the Shylock Group, much noted in the media
On the Rialto. Prompt recourse to the law
Fought off that one, and a great deal is owed
To our legal experts that we emerged unscathed,
Also leaner and fitter for the experience.

Now for the future: Our Private Finance Initiative
With the State of Venice and its noble Duke
Is off to an excellent start. We can thus provide
Substantial salary rises, options and bonuses
(Financial and in kind), all well-deserved,
To the directors, whose unswerving loyalty
Has seen us through an uncertain period.

I shall, if I may, end on a more personal note.
This has, for me, been a year of stress and trial.
I have been the unhappy subject of *such* quarrels!
They have taken their toll . . . I have seen the wilderness
And its beasts in another light . . . Am I, are any of us,
Better men (or women)? Will our deeds now shine
More brightly in a naughty world for this?

MICROCOSMS

The broken tape-end flap-flaps at the place
Where it snapped in mid-bar and left the ear empty.
Lots of days the same: left listening for a conclusion
That doesn't ever come, like this, like this –

Next day I saw, on a pavement alongside the Great
Highway of Life, a tail wagging a dog.
Though the specialty of dog had been neglected,
This hound was terribly proud of the strength of its tail.

My birthday comes round. After a meal, I tear
The dotted-line corner and release a sixteen-fold
Peculiarly cool and clammy refresher pad.
Does this mean I am still on an outgoing flight?

And then this doling-out, to the conscience-fretted,
With people taking and running, in all directions,
Their fists clenched round the coins in their little pockets
To keep them safe from other takers and runners.

I cancel the info-deficit on the screen
And look up at the mock-balustrade on this thirties bank.
So why this embellishment? Well, a balustrade was art,
And a bank was not. So it once thought it needed it.

Avoid smart ripostes on the phone. You can restart letters,
But never recall your phone-call apophthegms.
They will cling to someone else's memory like
A little dog in rhapsodies over an ankle.

No dodging the brutality of associations:
The arcade war-game playing a snatch of Webern,
The boys at the burger counter wearing surgeons' gowns,
My father's dead face driving the tube train home.

Though life still provides little leases: I press,
Then turn, the bulb in the rusty socket – it holds.
I step down, switch on – and it glows. This outcome
Was unforeseen in yesterday's Business Plan.

Or this image from a black-and-white film: a girl
Hears a bell ring and hurries to a bare brick wall
In a darkened garage; stops; lets it ring; saves
Her honour, as we hoped, with the unhooked receiver.

LEAVING THE WORLD OF PLEASURE

I gave up on the Mall of All Desires.
I thought it was pushing too much pleasure at me.

It was also other people's pleasure, thank you,
Not something I'd dreamed and chosen for myself.

They'd like to relaunch it for me, but they can't.
There's no new, lasting desire after twenty-five.

After the Mall, I saw the attraction of sorrow.
There was more scope in it for quenching old desires.

And it seemed to have a border, with happiness
On the unattainable other side of it.

INCIDENT ON A HOLIDAY

The cat between the tables is not worth attention,
But the most of *us* is closed in plastic now,
Magnetic so we stick to their powerful fingers.
I have to swipe to be a citizen.
I have to stand still while they target me.

Though one night on a coast of this vast and
Increasing inattention, a disco selling
Illusions to themselves for a sizeable profit
Goes up in flames in the small hours
– A blaze of interest on the coast opposite.

In this hinterland, however, no one explains it,
Not even the backstreet barber, the big
Conspiracy theorist, who avoids my eyes
In his pocked mirror; or the extrovert licensee
Working faster but very quietly, mopping his bar;

Not even the check-out girl taking one by one
The grapefruit rolled down in a ritual
To break the boredom of her dreadful day
And start her chatting – she doesn't as much as smile
When I ask her, 'Who would trash a lovely disco?'

– And claim the insurance on all the pretty dreams?
What sort of destructive decency? There was
No cc-tv watching, no bar code bleeped
When some unpoliced fingers scratched the match into flame.
And now there is a gap in the esplanade . . .

Though otherwise things go on pretty much the same:
The barber thanks me and tells me to Take Care,
The licensee puts my drink down – 'There you go!' –
The waters eject our pollution onto our shores,
And the cat, without e-mail, susses the customers

In the Sea Café, and refuses their burger bits.

KNOCK KNOCK

Do I need them? The glasses on my face?
The coat snatched to cover me? Not questions that I pose
Warm indoors while thinking *Nude is beautiful*,
But having unlocked the front door onto space,
And stared out into it to discover all
Of nobody there, and no neighbour to tell me whose

Loud knocking that might have been. I feel quite bold,
Because I don't shiver . . . Except I *can't*, my skin
Has suddenly felt content with nothing more
Than taking on, like clothes, the outer cold
– And the notion of re-shutting the opened door
Seems to be receding. With no one to let in,

I could go on standing in the freezing air
While my will to speak or move drained right away,
And the dark fastened hard on my illuminous
Nakedness. And then, if I called, 'Who's there?'
And heard – 'Bonaparte!' I'd say, 'Ridiculous!
Bonaparte *qui?*' . . . 'Bon appartement a louer.'